BLACK BEAR

NORTH AMERICA'S BEAR

STEPHEN R. SWINBURNE

BOYDS MILLS PRESS
HONESDALE, PENNSYLVANIA

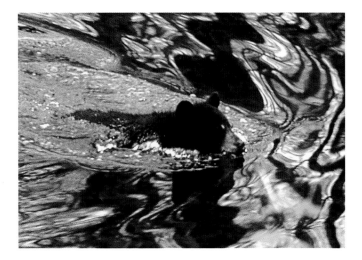

To my old friend Dennis McDermott and our literary heroes,
John Burroughs and Henry David Thoreau
— S. S.

I'm very grateful to the following black bear biologists and naturalists: Forrest Hammand, Ben Kilham, Alcott Smith, Sue Morse, and Mark Trenent. Thanks also to Gary Alt and Lynn Rogers for their books and lectures on black bears that proved so helpful in my research. I'm especially grateful to Dr. Lynn Rogers of the Wildlife Research Institute and North American Bear Center for reviewing the manuscript. Finally, many, many thanks to my friend Craig Dicken. Thanks for driving with me from Vermont to Pennsylvania to check bear dens in February. Your wonderful photographs at the bear den bring the chapter to life.

Photograph credits:
Steve Swinburne: Pages 25, 26, 30 top left, bottom left, top right
K. M. Anderson: Page 5 (bottom)
Craig Dicken: Pages 8-10, 12-15
Ben Kilham: Pages 3, 4, 6, 11, 16, 21-24, 27, 28-29, 30 (left, second photo; right, second and third photos), 31
Jerome Robinson: Page 26 (right)
National Park Service: Pages 17, 18, 19, 20
Yellowstone National Park: Page 5 (top)

Boyds Mills Press, Inc.
815 Church Street
Honesdale, Pennsylvania 18431
Printed in China

Library of Congress Cataloging-in-Publication Data

Swinburne, Stephen R.
    Black bear : North America's bear / by Stephen R. Swinburne. — 1st ed.
[48] p. : col. ill. , photos. ;   cm.
Includes index.
Summary: An examination of black bears, their behavior and habitat.
ISBN 978-1-59078-023-7 (hc)
ISBN 978-1-59078-798-4 (pb)
1. Black bear — Juvenile literature. 2. Bears — Juvenile literature. (1. Black bear. 2. Bears.)
I. Title.
599.74/ 446 21   QL737.C27S95 2003
2002117182

First edition
First Boyds Mills Press paperback edition, 2010
The text of this book is set in 13-point Garamond Book.

15 14 13 12 11 10 9 8 (hc)

10 9 8 7 6 5 4 3 2 (pb)

CONTENTS

Prologue

O<small>N A</small> <small>PEACEFUL</small> J<small>UNE</small> <small>EVENING</small> in the Adirondack Mountains of New York, I sit down with my family to a delicious lake trout dinner. Before I have a chance to take my first bite, a waiter shouts, "Look, a bear!"

About twenty people rush to a window overlooking the dining-room garden. We watch a black bear moving slowly but surely across the lawn to a bird feeder. The bear stands on its hind legs, then reaches up and bashes the feeder. The bear's first swipe brings the feeder crashing down, spilling seeds upon the ground. Dinner is served.

Quietly we ease open the dining-room door and gather on the porch to watch the bear, which is no more than thirty feet away.

"That's the third feeder I've hung in the last month," whispers the owner of the lodge. "Three strikes, I'm out. The bear wins. No more feeding the birds. Or bears!"

BLACK BEAR FACTS

Black bears come in many different colors. They can be black, brown, blonde, cinnamon, reddish, and all shades in between. Along certain parts of the British Columbia coast in Canada white black bears and blue black bears can even be found. Most black bears east of the Mississippi River are black, while most bears in the west are either black or brown. Black bears often show a splash of white on their chests; some individuals have a very definite white V. Within a family, black and brown cubs can occur.

black

brown

The bear hunkers low over the protein-rich sunflower seeds, shielding his booty like a child protecting a new toy. Sunflower seeds have twice the calories per gram of beech-nuts or acorns. The animal uses its long tongue to painstakingly extract the seeds from the mat of grass. We can hear the rhythmic chuffing of the bear's breathing and the contented sound of bear teeth chomping against seed. The bear remains still, head down, eating for nearly twenty minutes. Only once does it lift its head to look at us.

I continue watching the bear in the fading twilight. It's a beautiful animal—big, wild, and free. I've seen black bears many times in my life, but I'm always amazed at their size and power and how quickly they can move. Black bears can run fast—up to thirty miles per hour—for short periods. I remember driving a thickly wooded road in Vermont in early June when a half-mile up ahead I saw a large black bear. When I reached the place where the bear crossed the road, there was no sign of it. The forest had swallowed it whole. But on the other side of the road, where the bear had come from, there was plenty of sign of black bear. A massive beaver lodge the size of a large living room lay demolished. Logs and branches, thick and thin, lay strewn like a thrown fistful of pick-up sticks. I reasoned the bear had torn apart the lodge searching for young beavers to eat.

Eating. When a bear isn't sleeping or playing it's usually eating. It's one of the things bears do best. They eat whatever is available at different times of the year. Black bears will kill and eat small prey, such as deer fawns, and will also scavenge on animal carcasses. They relish ants and bees. Yet nuts (acorns, beechnuts), fruits (blueberries, raspberries, blackberries, apples, mountain ash), leaves, and roots form about 80 percent of a black bear's diet.

Our Adirondack bear has done a good job of vacuuming the spilled sunflower seeds from the ground. In the soft light from the lodge's windows I can see the bear finally move. It sniffs the ground for any missed seed. Then it turns and, led by its nose, saunters off into the forest.

Despite its teddy bear image and the raids on our backyard bird feeders and garbage cans, the black bear is at home in the woods. It is a wild creature that has evolved in its natural habitat over hundreds of thousands of years. The bear has lived here a lot longer than we have. Its home is in these Adirondack Mountains and in forests across much of North America. And as I go back to my trout dinner, I sense these woods are richer knowing that black bears live here. I may never see that bear again, but I'm happy knowing it's out there as my wild neighbor.

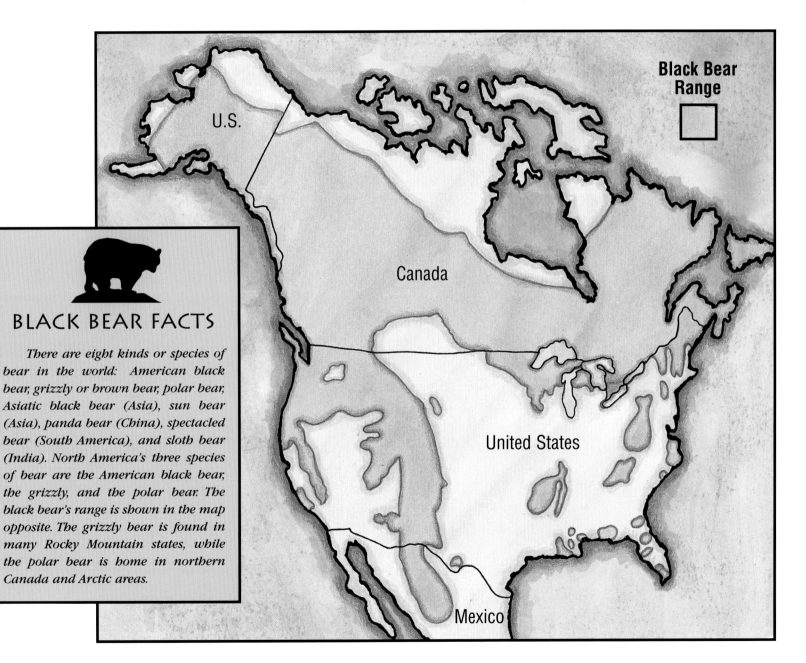

Black Bear Range

U.S.

Canada

United States

Mexico

BLACK BEAR FACTS

There are eight kinds or species of bear in the world: American black bear, grizzly or brown bear, polar bear, Asiatic black bear (Asia), sun bear (Asia), panda bear (China), spectacled bear (South America), and sloth bear (India). North America's three species of bear are the American black bear, the grizzly, and the polar bear. The black bear's range is shown in the map opposite. The grizzly bear is found in many Rocky Mountain states, while the polar bear is home in northern Canada and Arctic areas.

Chapter One

My First Bear Cubs

WE LOOK HARD INTO A HUGE BRUSH PILE fifty feet from where we stand. I can't see a thing, but I hear bear cubs. The property owner has led a half dozen people, mostly wildlife biologists, to a bear den in a section of pretty woods not far from his house in northeastern Pennsylvania on a cold, late-February day. A friend and I from Vermont have come along to watch and learn.

Mark Trenent, Pennsylvania's bear biologist, and three other naturalists approach the brush pile cautiously with loaded rifles. These rifles are armed with tranquilizer darts, not bullets. One person carries a long aluminum jab stick also fitted with a dart. The biologists surround the brush pile in case the sow, the adult female, decides to run.

"Most times the sow stays put," says Mark. "But black bears are unpredictable. We want to try to tranquilize her in case she bolts. If she gets away, she could abandon the young and we'd have orphan cubs on our hands."

While the biologists spread out, Mark crawls into the brush pile with the jab stick. As he disappears from sight, the bear cubs start squalling. Five minutes later, Mark reappears and confers with the others. Another biologist goes into the brush pile, again the cubs start squalling, and, a few moments later, the biologist emerges. Lots of heads start to shake. I stamp my feet to keep them from freezing. After an hour of trying to dart the mother bear, the biologists give up. As we head back to our cars, Mark explains that the sow had dug a hole under the brush and was too difficult to tranquilize and move. I feel my spirits sink and I wonder if we will see a bear today.

Fortunately Mark has lined up another den check for the afternoon. After a quick bite to eat and a short drive, we pull off the road and park in an open stand of woods and shrubs. Mark and another biologist walk across the road with the tranquilizer darts. Within fifteen minutes they return and announce, "She's down. You can go in."

We cross the road and plunge up a wooded rise and find the bear den, just a hole in the ground, a few feet from a large lake. I'm amazed at how unprotected this site appears.

One of the best ways for scientists to gauge the number of black bear cubs born each year is to check their dens. Wildlife biologists prepare to tranquilize the mother bear with an aluminum jab stck or rifle fitted with darts.

BLACK BEAR FACTS

Do bears hibernate? It depends on which scientist you ask. Many hibernation researchers say bears do hibernate, while some say bears are not true hibernators. They say woodchucks and bats are real hibernators, as their body temperatures and heart rates drop very low during hibernation. Some scientists believe bears might be considered semi-hibernators because their temperature drops only a degree or two. And while their heart rate can fall as low as eight beats per minute when they are in a deep sleep, it can beat as fast as one hundred times a minute when the sow is nursing young. Despite the ongoing debate about hibernation, everyone agrees black bears undergo an amazing change that allows them to survive through the winter.

Bears eat almost nonstop in the fall, consuming as many as twenty thousand calories a day (the same number of calories in forty-two hamburgers!). They enter the dens with thick layers of body fat and survive the winter by living off this stored fat. While in the den, black bears don't eat, don't defecate, and don't urinate. Scientists have discovered that bears can convert or change urea into protein. This allows them to maintain their muscle tone throughout the winter sleep.

Bear den

Feeding on a deer

We are about 150 feet from a fairly busy two-lane highway, and yet mother bear has hibernated here.

Mark explains that he used a nine-foot extendable pole fitted with a tranquilizer drug to dart the sow. It takes ten to twenty minutes for the bear to become sedated, or fall asleep. She will be out for about two hours.

When Mark is confident the bear is peacefully dozing, he shimmies down into the den hole. I lean in and Mark hands me a squirming, bawling black bear cub. I no sooner have the one cub tucked under my arm when up comes another. I nestle the cubs into my fleece jacket to keep them warm. They settle down as I sit in the sunshine and watch Mark and the other biologists work on the sow.

Mark ties a rope to her front paws and they haul her from the den. They stretch her on her side on a sleeping bag. Mark squeezes two or three drops of ointment in the bear's eyes to keep them moist. He throws his pair of gloves over her face. The bear can't blink due to the tranquilizer, and her eyes could dry and become damaged. Mark's eye drops prevent this, and the gloves protect her eyes from the light.

He then pulls up her upper lip, showing a set of numbers that were tattooed on her inside cheek when she was first captured. This is Bear #10395. The same number is on the first set of ear tags placed on the bear and will stay with the bear throughout its life. Mark records the number. Later, after checking his database, his computer reveals the biologists know a lot about #10395. She was first captured

I reach in to take the first of two cubs from Mark.

Biologists haul 256 pounds of sleeping mother bear from the den.

While three biologists carry the sow to weigh her ...

Mark's gloves protect the sow's eyes from the sun.

I cuddle with the five-pound, seven-week-old cubs to keep them warm.

and tagged in June 1994, when a biologist learned the bear was two years old. Number 10395 was recaptured in 1995 and fixed with a radio collar. Biologists lost track of her between 1996 and 1998, most likely because her collar fell off. In May 1999, she was recaptured and a new collar put on. In 2000, #10395 had cubs. She had cubs again in 2002. Mark believes this is her third or fourth litter.

After recording her lip tattoo, Mark makes sure her ear tags are secure. He checks her overall condition, monitoring her vital signs. He checks for mange, a skin disease, which has infected some Pennsylvania bears. With the help of three other biologists, we weigh #10395. Mark says the records show that this female bear's weight has gone up and down according to the season. She weighed 158 pounds in June 1994 and then 302 pounds in October 1995. Today she weighs 256 pounds. I dig my hands into the sow's luxurious coat and grab rolls of fat. This bear is in good shape.

With the work on the sow complete, Mark turns his attention to the cubs. At about seven weeks old they have no teeth. Their claws, though, are grappling hooks. They climb on me like I'm a jungle gym. In his field book, Mark records the sex (both males) and weight (five pounds each). He places metal ear tags into a set of pliers and says, "Hang onto the cubs." Mark works the bear's ears between the pliers and squeezes. The cub lets out a deafening yelp but a moment later is quiet. We tag the other three ears, and the numbers on the ear tags are recorded.

I give my furry friend one last bear hug before he rejoins his brother and mom in the den.

The cubs at seven weeks old have cut no teeth and naturally suck my finger.

I snuggle with a newly tagged cub.

Mark says most bear den checks take about two hours, and we've been here about that long. It's time to return the mother bear to the den. The goal of a bear biologist is to put the family back the way he or she found them. Once the sow is lying in the den comfortably curled on her side, I pass Mark one of the cubs. He tucks him alongside the mother's warm stomach. I hold the remaining cub up and take a long last look. I hate to let go of my little furry friend. Tucked into my arm, I feel like I'm holding my favorite teddy bear. Finally I unhinge the baby bear's tiny hooks. Mark nestles the cub beside his brother. Within minutes the cubs are nursing. We step quietly away from the den, leaving the family of bears in peace.

NATURE DICTIONARY

Defecate: to pass waste
Mange: skin disease caused by parasites
Mortality: the death of a living organism
Scat: an animal's feces
Sow: an adult female bear
Tranquilizer: a drug that makes an animal go to sleep temporarily
Urea: the liquid waste or urine of an animal
Urinate: to discharge urine

BLACK BEAR FACTS

Bear #10395 was born in 1992. She was ten years old in 2002. Another bear from the same county (Pike County in northeastern Pennsylvania) reached thirty years of age. "While there are documented cases of bears in other states living as long if not longer," says Mark Trenent, Pennsylvania's bear biologist, "this thirty-year-old female bear is the oldest bear we have confirmed living in the wilds of Pennsylvania." Mark says females can have cubs right up to old age. Primary bear mortality includes hunting and highway deaths. Cars on Pennsylvania's roads kill about three hundred bears each year. Bears are also destroyed if they become a nuisance. Lynn L. Rogers, renowned bear biologist from Minnesota, states, "Black bears can live twenty-one to thirty-three years or more."

Chapter Two

DON'T FEED THE BEARS

A worker feeds a black bear in Yellowstone Park sometime in the early twentieth century.

ON A BEAUTIFUL BLUE-SKY DAY, we watch black bears from the car. Omega Park is a wild game preserve in Montebello, Canada, halfway between Montreal and Quebec. For half an hour we've watched a sow and her two cubs feed and play and be bears in a large chainlink enclosure. We do not get out of the car and have parked at least forty feet away from the fenced-in bears.

People love watching bears. America's love affair with bears began in Yellowstone, this country's first national park, created in 1872. Feeding the bears in Yellowstone was almost a national pastime for over fifty years.

Bears pick through the rubbish for tasty bits in Yellowstone Park in the early twentieth century.

But watching bears used to be very different than it is today. Imagine driving into Yellowstone in 1952, with a bag of bread and a jar of peanut butter. You're so excited. You're going to feed the bears.

It started when Yellowstone began building its first hotels to accommodate park visitors. Hotel garbage was disposed of in open pits nearby. It wasn't long before bears discovered the refuse. By 1889, black bears were gathering in the evening at the heaps of garbage. At the same time, tourists began gathering at the dumps to watch the bears. A nice arrangement began — bears learned that man was a

A splendid show is guaranteed for all: Tourists watch bears feed at a garbage dump in Yellowstone Park more than eighty years ago.

Sometimes the seven o'clock "bear talk" at Old Faithful in Yellowstone Park was packed with nearly three thousand people. While a National Park Service ranger gave a talk on bears, the crowds watched up to a dozen or more grizzlies sort through piles of trash. Photo taken sometime in the 1920s.

source of food through his garbage, and man learned that garbage attracted bears and bears were fun to watch.

In 1903, President Theodore "Teddy" Roosevelt was on vacation and visited Yellowstone to see the bears. The year before, Roosevelt, an avid sportsman, was hunting in Mississippi. During that trip, he encountered a small black bear, which he refused to shoot. The episode of the young bear being spared by the President's rifle inspired the teddy bear, one of America's most-loved toys.

By the 1920s, bear feeding had become a major Yellowstone attraction. About ten thousand people came to Yellowstone between 1872 and 1882. By 1929, Yellowstone had up to 260,000 visitors per year. A lot more visitors meant a lot more garbage, and more garbage meant more bears. On a good night in the 1920s, you could sit in the stands at the Old Faithful bear feeding grounds and see as many as fifty to seventy black and grizzly bears. Bears sorted through garbage strewn about on wooden platforms. A National Park Service ranger, mounted on a horse, spoke to the crowd about the bears.

As traffic increased in Yellowstone, bears discovered a new way to get food—beg for it. During the 1920s, bears waited for handouts along park roads. Visitors to the park during the 1950s and 1960s remember regularly seeing thirty or more bears along park roads begging for food. Sometimes a "bear jam" would back up traffic as tourists waited for a chance to see and feed the bears. Yellowstone visitors went to great lengths to photograph their children with black bears. Children were told to stand by the bear and sometimes were even slathered in honey and jelly so the bear could be photographed licking it off. Kids were even plonked on a bear's back and asked to smile for the camera.

With humans in such close contact with these wild creatures, bear-caused injuries increased. Yellowstone National Park recorded that bears injured an average of forty-eight people a year during the period of 1931-1959. Bears don't know where the candy bar ends and a hand begins. In 1960, the park began efforts to reduce garbage sources and handouts of food from visitors. But it wasn't until 1970 that Yellowstone declared it was eliminating all sources of human food and garbage in the park. Biologists and park officials agreed that offering human food to bears was dangerous and unhealthy for the bears as well as people. The goal of the program was to restore both black and grizzly bears to a diet of natural food. Since 1983, bear-caused human injuries have declined to an average of one per year. When you go to Yellowstone or Yosemite or the Great Smoky Mountains or any of our other national parks these days, you don't feed the bears—they feed themselves.

Though bears are protected in places like Yellowstone, there are many places where bears have no protection. Right now, somewhere in the United States, a bulldozer is flattening a section of forest. The trees will be cleared, a

A bear jam in progress: Black bears begging for handouts was a common sight in Yellowstone during the 1950s and 1960s.

BLACK BEAR FACTS

Black bears usually mate from late May to early July. The sow gives birth to anywhere from one to five cubs, usually two or three, in January. The newborn bears are blind, toothless, and covered in fine dark hair. The cubs weigh about a half-pound to a pound at birth, and after nursing on mother's rich milk, they emerge from the den in mid-April weighing around ten pounds. The bear family will stay together through the summer and into the fall. The cubs watch their mother's every move and learn by imitating her. The family will hibernate come winter. The following summer the cubs go their own way, and the sow is again ready to breed. Most black bears breed for the first time when they are between three and seven years old and raise one litter every two years. The boars, or males, play no role in raising the young.

Sow and cubs

foundation poured, and a house will rise. The forest that was destroyed was not empty. A bear lived there. The forest was the bear's home. And when the family barbecues and leaves corncobs, half-eaten hamburger rolls, and bits of apple pie in the garbage, a bear may visit. It may spill the trash and finish the barbecue. Right now, somewhere in the United States, a homeowner living on the edge of a large forest is filling a bird feeder with sunflower seeds. Sometime after dark, while the family sleeps, a black bear may come and pull apart the bird feeder and eat the seeds.

People need to become smarter about living with black bears. When people build their homes in bear country or feed birds where bears live, bears may become a nuisance. Bears think a lot about eating. Tie down or put away the trash cans. Don't feed the birds in summer if bears come calling for birdseed. Outsmart the bears.

Chapter Three

SCHOOLTIME FOR BEARS

It's May and time for young bears to go to school. For orphaned bears in New Hampshire, there's no better teacher than Ben Kilham.

Ben is a woodsman, naturalist, and licensed wildlife rehabilitator from Lyme, New Hampshire. In 1993, he received two orphaned bear cubs and for fifteen months took on the duties of feeding, sheltering, protecting, and guiding them.

"Hi, guys. Hi, guys," says Ben as we walk quietly up to two young bears in a large cage on Ben's eighty-acre lot deep in the New Hampshire forest.

Since his first parenting experience in 1993, Ben has raised over thirty-five black bear cubs. He has released them all into the wild. Ben doesn't raise cubs in the conventional way, keeping them in a cage. He establishes a very close bond with the young bears and then brings the bears up in the most natural environment possible. That means he takes them for walks in the woods, he plays with them, vocalizes with them, cuddles up and takes naps with them. He becomes a mother bear.

Most of the bears Ben receives are cubs, sometimes as young as five to seven weeks old. When the bears are this young, Ben is able to quickly gain their trust and he handles them without hesitation. The bears we are now visiting are yearlings. Their mother was killed during hunting season and they needed a home. When bears need help, Ben Kilham is there to help them.

When we first arrive, the bears retreat to the rear of the pen, eyeing us suspiciously. But Ben coaxes them closer with gentle, soothing words.

"It's okay, c'mon now. It's okay, guys. You're okay," Ben says softly to the bears.

Ben visits these bears every day; they know him. I'm the stranger, and the young bears put on a show of threatening behavior.

The larger of the two bears, bigger than a German shepherd, comes slowly toward me in a stiff-legged walk with his head bowed down. He's chomping his jaws,

Biologist Ben Kilham and three of his students.

A young bear rises to introduce himself to me with a bear stare and squared-off lips.

making a sound like two wooden blocks being knocked together. At about three feet away, he explodes into an upright stance, coming a foot from my face. A wall of wire separates us. The bear huffs in my face and squares off his lips.

And then, as quickly as it began, the display is over. The bear drops to all fours and wanders off calmly for a drink of water in a big green plastic barrel.

"This is common behavior when bears meet other

bears. They also do it when they encounter a strange person," says Ben. "The stiff-legged walk, chomping jaws, huffing, bluff charges, and squared-off lip, all this behavior may look like aggression, but it's the bear's way of communicating, testing their social dominance. I've been charged hundreds of times like that and with no wire between the bear and me. The best thing to do is to stand your ground, keep your eyes on the bear. Let the bear do its thing, and wait for the display to end. As it always does in a minute or so."

To establish a mutual trust, Ben spends hours and hours in the woods hanging out with the bears.

"It's okay. C'mon guy, you're okay," says Ben Kilham softly as he works closer to the yearling cub.

26

Ben believes one of the biggest misconceptions about black bears is their mean temper when their young are present. He tells me that of the dozen or so times he's run into wild sows with cubs, the sow always retreats. Flight rather than fight is the black bear's rule. Grizzly bears, on the other hand, will aggressively defend their young.

After our visit with the young bears, Ben takes me on a walk to look for bear sign. He shows me a small woodland pond where bears like to come in the dog days of August to cool off. We inspect a red pine tree with bite holes and claw marks and tufts of bear hair stuck in pinesap. He shows me where the bears' supermarket grows—wild lettuce, jack-in-the-pulpit, beechnut, and black cherry. He knows these woods. If I were an orphaned black bear cub, I'd be in good hands with Ben Kilham.

Chapter Four

LOOKING FOR SIGN OF BEAR

IF YOU SPEND SOME TIME IN THE WOODS, you may be lucky enough to see a bear. But you're more likely to see black bear sign than the actual bear. Try to read the stories left by the bear's tracks and sign. What was the bear doing? Where was it going? Who knows, the next time you tramp these woods, over the next rise may wait your first encounter with the American black bear. Here's what to look for:

Claw marks

Scat

Tracks

BEAR CLAW MARKS: If you're in black bear country, look for beech trees. Bears eat beechnuts and climb the tree to gorge on nuts in the canopy. When they climb, their claws dig into the smooth gray trunk, leaving tell-tale claw marks. These are easy sign of bears to find. If this is a favorite bear-feeding tree, over time the bark of the tree may record the claw marks of many climbing bears.

Beech and other trees offer another clue. They are like billboards for bears. They rub themselves against the bark to leave messages for other bears. Look for bear hair stuck on bark or patches of sap.

BEAR SCAT: Bears are omnivorous, eating both plants and animals, so their scat can look different depending on what they eat. If a bear has eaten blueberries or beechnuts, it's easy to tell because their scat is full of fruit or nut pieces.

BEAR TRACKS: The tracks of adult black bears can be about five to seven inches long, and show five toes on their front and rear feet along with front and rear palm and heel pads. Sometimes you can see their claw marks.

BEAR NESTS: Look up into the crown of American beech, black cherry, wild apple, and oak trees in late August and September, and you may see a bear nest. This marks where a bear has climbed the tree, sat in the crown, and fed. The bear bends all the fruit- or nut-laden branches toward it in a big pile for easy feeding.

BEAR LOGS OR ROCKS: Bears tear apart logs, searching for delicious ants and larvae to eat. Bears also turn over rocks, looking for grubs, ants, or other insects. Search the rock for scratch marks from the bear's claws.

Nest

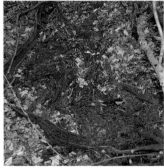

Splinters from torn log

Bears are one of the most exciting animals to see in the woods. You'll probably always remember your first encounter with a wild bear. I remember mine. I was visiting the Great Smoky Mountains National Park with my college zoology class during spring break. I was out front, leading the class through a beautiful glade of Appalachian woods filled with spring birds and spring wildflowers. We came over a small hill, and on the trail about thirty feet ahead of us we saw a black bear. The bear rose to its hind legs, as if to get a better look at us, then dropped to all four feet and vanished into the brush and was gone. The sighting lasted five seconds but the memory, a lifetime.

High on a beech-covered ridge in southern Vermont on a late September day, I pause in my walk from the summit and kneel in the leafy sunshine. The silence of the woods is awesome. I can hear my heart beat. I can hear a leaf fall. I gather up a fistful of beechnuts. And, in a silly, hiking-solo moment, I offer them up in my outstretched palm to the nearest bear in earshot. "Here, bear. Here, bear." No bear comes, of course. So I work the beechnuts into a pile and offer a hushed blessing: May beechnuts always be on your path. May these mountains always shelter you and your generations. May you live long, bear, and may your cubs be strong.

Further Reading

While doing research for this book, I discovered many good books about black bears. *Bears* (Nature Fact File) by Michael Bright (Southwater, Anness Publishing Inc., 2002) and *Black Bears* (Our Wild World Series) by Kathy Feeney (Creative Publishing International, 2000) provide a lot of fascinating facts. I also recommend two books that may interest older readers. *Among the Bears* by Ben Kilham (Henry Holt and Company, 2002) is a wonderful story about a man who becomes mother bear and raises orphaned cubs. *Tracking and the Art of Seeing: How to Read Animal Tracks and Sign* by Paul Rezendes (Camden House Publishing, Inc., 1995) includes a great chapter on black bear tracks and sign. You can also check out the following Web sites on bears:

www.bearden.org

www.bear.org

www.americanbear.org

You can learn more about black bears and other animals on my Web site:
www.steveswinburne.com

INDEX